WORLD BOOK'S
LIBRARY OF NATURAL DISASTERS

ICE STORMS

WORLD BOOK

a Scott Fetzer company
Chicago
www.worldbookonline.com

World Book, Inc.
233 N. Michigan Avenue
Chicago, IL 60601
U.S.A.

For information about other World Book publications, visit our Web site at
http://www.worldbookonline.com or call **1-800-WORLDBK (967-5325)**.

For information about sales to schools and libraries, call **1-800-975-3250 (United States);
1-800-837-5365 (Canada)**.

2008 revised printing

Library of Congress Cataloging-in-Publication Data

Ice storms.
     p. cm. -- (World Book's library of natural disasters)
     Summary: "A discussion of a major type of natural
disaster, including descriptions of some of the most
destructive; explanations of these phenomena, what
causes them, and where they occur; and information
about how to prepare for and survive these forces of
nature. Features include an activity, glossary, list of
resources, and index"--Provided by publisher.
     Includes bibliographical references and index.
     ISBN 978-0-7166-9809-8
     1. Ice storms--Juvenile literature.
     2. Natural disasters--Juvenile literature.
     I. World Book, Inc.
     QC926.37.I24 2007
     551.55'6--dc22
                              2007006684

World Book's Library of Natural Disasters
Set ISBN: 978-0-7166-9801-2

Printed in China
2 3 4 5 6 12 11 10 09 08

Editor in Chief: Paul A. Kobasa

Supplementary Publications
    Associate Director: Scott Thomas
    Managing Editor: Barbara A. Mayes

Editors: Jeff De La Rosa, Nicholas Kilzer,
    Christine Sullivan, Kristina A. Vaicikonis,
    Marty Zwikel

Researchers: Cheryl Graham, Jacqueline Jasek

Manager, Editorial Operations
    (Rights & Permissions): Loranne K. Shields

Graphics and Design
    Associate Director: Sandra M. Dyrlund
    Associate Manager, Design: Brenda B. Tropinski
    Associate Manager, Photography: Tom Evans
    Designer: Matt Carrington

Product development: Arcturus Publishing Limited
Writers: Anna Claybourne, Barbara A. Mayes
Editors: Nicola Barber, Alex Woolf
Designer: Jane Hawkins
Illustrator: Stefan Chabluk

Acknowledgments:

AP Photo: 11 (Joe Hermosa), 38 (Stephen Holman), 42 Larry W. Smith, 43 (Seth Perlman).

Corbis: 5 (Alexander Natruskin/ Reuters), 8, 9 (Larry W. Smith/ epa), 10 (Bob Daemmrich/ Bob Daemmrich
    Photography, Inc.), 15, 27, 29, 32 (Christopher Morris), 18 (Bettmann), 21 (epa), 23 (John McAnulty), 28 (Poulina
    Pierre Paul/ Corbis Sygma), 30 (Macduff Everton), 31 (Perry Mastrovito), 33, 34 (Reuters), 36 (Winter Damon/
    Corbis Sygma), 37 (Buddy Mays), 39 (Image Source), 41 (Visuals Unlimited).

Getty Images: 4 (Larry W. Smith), 14 (Ravell Call/ Liaison), 35 (Robert Laberge/ AFP).

Nashville Public Library: 17 (The Nashville Room).

Peter Arnold, Inc.: cover/ title page (Gene Rhoden).

Science Photo Library: 6, 19 (Ted Kinsman), 7 (Dr Juerg Alean), 20 (Claus Lunau/ Bonnier Publications),
    40 (Mark Burnett).

TOPEX/ Poseidon, NASA JPL: 25.

TABLE OF CONTENTS

Glossary There is a glossary of terms on pages 45-46. Terms defined in the glossary are in type **that looks like this** on their first appearance on any spread (two facing pages).

Additional resources Books for further reading and recommended Web sites are listed on page 47. Because of the nature of the Internet, some Web site addresses may have changed since publication. The publisher has no responsibility for any such changes or for the content of cited sources.

A pickup truck drives down an icy road surrounded by frozen trees during an ice storm in Wichita, Kansas, in 2005.

An ice storm is one of the most dangerous types of winter storm. During an ice storm, roads, **utility** lines, and other outdoor surfaces and objects become coated with slippery ice. The United States National Weather Service issues a warning for an ice storm if **meteorologists** predict that ice will build up to a depth of at least ¼ inch (0.6 centimeter).

Ice storms rarely injure or kill people directly. Instead, they cut people off from the warmth, water, and food they need to survive. They also make walking and driving perilous.

Icy glitter

During an ice storm, the ice itself doesn't fall from the sky, like snow. Instead, the ice forms when very cold rain—known as **freezing rain**—falls onto cold surfaces and freezes instantly. Everything exposed to the rain becomes covered in ice. Sidewalks, trees, street signs—even cars left outside—become covered by glimmering ice.

Ice storm dangers

Ice storms can be as hazardous as they are beautiful. They turn roads and sidewalks into skating rinks. The ice drags down and breaks power and telephone lines. It wreaks havoc on trees, weighing down and snapping branches—and often sending them crashing onto utility lines. Ice build-up can cause roofs to collapse.

Ice storms often claim lives. People die because of injuries suffered in traffic accidents and falls and from **hypothermia.** People also die because they rely on heaters not designed for indoor use that give off deadly **fumes** or catch fire.

A MODERN THREAT

Ice storms are probably more dangerous now than they were 100 years ago. The electric-powered conveniences that supply our heat and light and the roadways, railways, and other modern transportation systems that we depend on, especially in **urban** areas, have made people more vulnerable to an ice storm's damaging effects. Buying food and other necessities may be difficult because without electric power, cash registers, credit-card payment systems, and cash machines shut down.

In 2004, the glass roof of a sports center in Moscow, Russia, collapsed from the weight of ice and snow that had built up on top of it.

Where and when?

Ice storms occur in many parts of the world, but they are most frequent and severe in the United States and Canada. Major ice storms usually strike North America about once every two to three years.

Ice storms usually develop from late November through early May. They rarely happen in the coldest weather, however. Ice storms are most likely to occur when the air temperature is around or just below **freezing point** (32 °F [0 °C]). The actual storm may last for only a few hours or days, but the effects of the storm may linger for weeks or even months.

FROZEN SOLID

The ice that forms during an ice storm is usually smooth—an especially dangerous characteristic. Because **freezing rain** is still a liquid when it hits the ground, it coats surfaces in fairly even layers as it hardens. Freezing rain also sticks strongly to the surfaces it touches—another dangerous characteristic—because its **molecules** strongly bond to the molecules of other substances. **Meteorologists** categorize the ice that forms from freezing rain as **glaze** or **rime.**

Glaze

Glaze appears almost clear, like glass. Glaze is heavier than snow, frost, or rime because it forms from raindrops, rather than the crystals that make up most other types of frozen water. When glaze forms on highways and streets, it is popularly known as **black ice.** From certain angles, black ice appears as a dark patch on the surface. Often, however, black ice is all but invisible, a peril for both drivers and pedestrians.

WHY IS ICE SLIPPERY?

It's hard to stay upright while walking on an icy sidewalk or to steer a car while driving over an icy roadway. Ice is slippery because even at temperatures slightly below freezing, a thin layer of liquid water remains on the surface of the ice. The molecules in this liquidlike layer are arranged in a jumbled way, and they vibrate rapidly. As a result, the surface layer acts as a **lubricant,** reducing the **friction** that would be created by shoes or tires on a dry surface.

During an ice storm, power lines may become coated in heavy glaze.

Rime

Rime, which looks like heavy **frost,** forms from tiny raindrops. These raindrops freeze more quickly than those that form glaze. As the tiny raindrops freeze, small pockets of air become trapped between them. These air pockets make rime lighter than glaze. They also make the ice appear grainy and milky-white rather than transparent. The air pockets prevent rime from clinging to surfaces as stubbornly as glaze does, and so rime generally causes less damage.

How thick? How heavy?

Glaze can become amazingly thick. During a severe storm, glaze may build up on roadways and roofs to a thickness of 6 inches (15 centimeters) or more. The ice may also encase electric-power lines, boosting their diameter to as much as 2 inches (5 centimeters). Ice this thick adds an extra 65 pounds (29 kilograms) to each yard (meter) of the line. It is no surprise that **utility** lines sag or even break under such a burden. A 50-foot (15-meter) conifer (cone-bearing tree) may accumulate as much as 99,000 pounds (45,000 kilograms) of ice during a severe storm—an amount equal to the weight of about 50 elephants.

A thick build-up of rime on pillars is formed into dramatic shapes by the wind.

THE NORTH AMERICAN ICE STORMS OF 2007

Waves of crippling ice storms—often mixed with snow, arctic temperatures, and **blizzard-**force winds—battered a huge section of the United States from Texas to Maine as well as parts of southeastern Canada in January 2007. The storms claimed at least 85 lives in 12 states and 3 provinces. At least 400,000 people were forced to battle the dangerous winter weather without electric power. Oklahoma, Texas, and Missouri bore the brunt of the storms, which struck in three waves beginning on Friday, January 12.

The enormous weight of ice splits a tree in McAlester, Oklahoma, right down the middle.

Oklahoma

The **freezing rain** struck eastern Oklahoma hardest of all, leaving up to 4 inches (10 centimeters) of ice in some places. Authorities there reported at least 25 storm-related deaths, more than half of them from traffic accidents. Seven of the victims died in one accident, after their van collided with a truck that slid into incoming traffic. At least 110,000 people were left in the cold and darkness as ice-coated tree branches snapped and fell onto power lines. One week after the storm hit, more than 20,000 homes and

TREE DEVASTATION

The ice crushed thousands of trees in eastern Oklahoma. "It looks like Godzilla came through there and just stomped them all down," said one Oklahoman describing the damage to his neighborhood.

businesses in the state were still without electric power—despite the efforts of **utility** crews working around the clock—and many people had fled to temporary shelters.

Problems in McAlester

The town of McAlester in southeastern Pittsburg County, Oklahoma, endured more than its share of hardship. Up to 90 percent of its 18,000 residents lost power after the storm hit on January 12. Ice as thick as 1 to 2 inches (3 to 5 centimeters) covered the power lines and caused 900 utility poles to collapse. On January 19, a major transmission line broke, plunging the rest of McAlester and many surrounding communities into darkness for most of the day. Pittsburg County officials ordered a nighttime **curfew** to prevent motorists from running into downed power lines in the dark. They also hoped to halt the theft of emergency **generators** placed along railroad crossings to power safety gates. On January 22, some 1,200 residents were still waiting to have their power restored, though warmer temperatures and rain made the work of nearly 1,000 electric utility workers much easier.

Ice-coated power lines hang threateningly over an Oklahoma highway in the aftermath of a major ice storm that swept through a number of Midwestern states in January 2007, leaving tens of thousands of people without power.

In addition to crippling large areas of Oklahoma, the 2007 ice storms pummeled parts of Texas and Missouri. They also struck sections of Arkansas, Illinois, Indiana, Iowa, Kansas, Maine, Michigan, Nebraska, New Hampshire, New York, North Carolina, and South Carolina. In Canada, **freezing rain** closed schools and highways in parts of Ontario, Nova Scotia, and New Brunswick.

Texas troubles

In Texas, freezing rain covered the roads in ice as far south as San Antonio. Officials in Texas reported at least 10 storm-related deaths, some resulting from **carbon monoxide** poisoning. The storms paralyzed the state's transportation systems. Hundreds of flights were cancelled at airports in Austin, San Antonio, and the Dallas-Fort Worth area as workers struggled to de-ice planes and runways. Freezing rain and ice shut down 300 miles (483 kilometers) of Interstate 10 between Fort Stockton and San Antonio for two days. In the state capital, Austin, freezing rain forced Governor Rick Perry to move his inaugural ceremony indoors and cancel his inaugural parade.

Fringes of ice decorate chairs set up for Texas Governor Rick Perry's outdoor inauguration ceremony in Austin, the state capital, in January 2007. The ice forced Perry to move the ceremony indoors.

TOASTY TEXAS TURTLES

During the storms, volunteers in southeastern Texas rescued at least 150 sea turtles stunned by plunging water temperatures in the Gulf of Mexico. As the turtles washed ashore, volunteers—spearheaded by the conservation group Sea Turtle, Inc.—wrapped the cold-blooded **reptiles** in blankets and towels and rushed them to several shelters, where they were revived by heat lamps and lettuce. Without rescue, the turtles would likely have died from the cold or would have become easy targets for **predators.**

Missouri misery

In Missouri, the ice storms claimed at least 14 victims and knocked out power to as many as 325,000 people, most of them in the Springfield and St. Louis areas. Missouri Governor Matt Blunt declared a statewide emergency and sent National Guard troops into the hardest-hit areas to help clear roads and check on residents. Amtrak officials halted train services between Kansas City and St. Louis for two days as crews struggled to clear railroad tracks of trees and branches damaged by the ice.

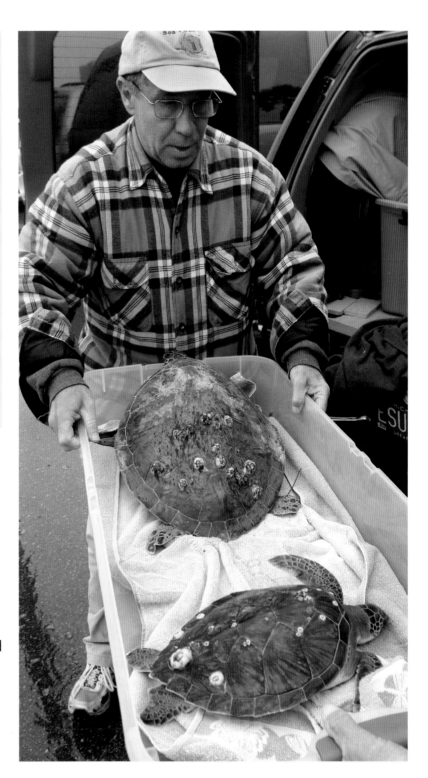

Conservation workers carry sea turtles to safety after rescuing them from the cold on the Texan shoreline in January 2007. They were returned to the wild in February.

Ice storms develop only when three essential weather elements—subfreezing air, above-freezing air, and plenty of moisture—come together in a certain way. Fortunately, these elements and conditions are so specific that severe ice storms are relatively rare.

Warm air, cold air

Ice storms and nearly all other weather occur in the lowest layer of Earth's **atmosphere.** There, large volumes of air called **air masses** continually rise and fall and move horizontally over the planet's surface. Cold air masses tend to sink because they are **dense**—that is, their **molecules** are closely packed together. In contrast, warm air is less dense and so it tends to rise.

Water vapor

The atmosphere contains **water vapor** that has evaporated from seas, rivers, and soil and been given off by plant leaves. Warm air

Warm and cold air masses over North America and the Atlantic Ocean typically move in set patterns around the world. An ice storm can occur when warm and cold air masses meet and overlap.

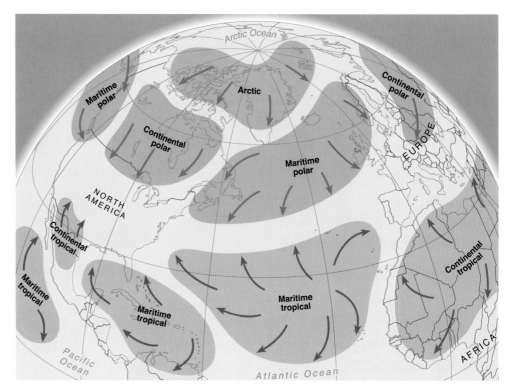

holds more water vapor than cold air. As warm air cools, its water vapor **condenses** into droplets, which appear as clouds. The droplets combine and fall as rain, snow, hail, or **sleet,** all of which are **precipitation**.

Cold air, warm air

During the winter, dry air masses at temperatures at or below **freezing point** often flow from snow-covered regions of northern Canada into the eastern or southern regions of Canada and the United States. These air masses, which are relatively thin, tend to sink and hug the surface. Because the cold air is so dense, it resists being moved along by incoming **weather systems** and so may settle in an area for days or weeks. Also in the winter, masses of warmer air carrying moisture flow north and east from the Gulf of Mexico.

Meeting and mixing over North America

Because of the way air masses meet and mix above North America, the eastern part of the continent is more likely to experience ice storms than any other area of the world. Ice-storm weather begins with an entrenched, surface-hugging mass of cold air. If warmer, vapor-laden air from the Gulf of Mexico moves into the same area, it is forced up and over the cold layer. Because the air high above the surface is also cold, the warm air ends up being "sandwiched" between two cold layers.

An ice storm occurs when snow falls through a layer of warm air and melts into rain, then meets a layer of very cold air close to the ground. It freezes on contact with the cold surface of the ground and other objects.

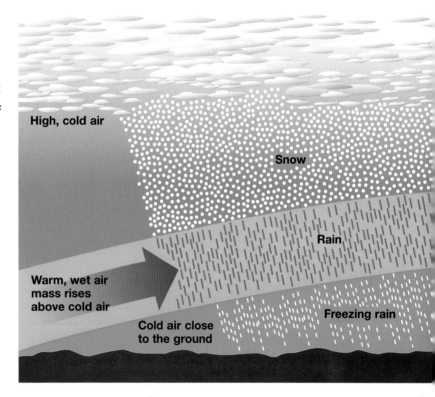

High, cold air

Snow

Rain

Warm, wet air mass rises above cold air

Cold air close to the ground

Freezing rain

ROCKY MOUNTAIN BLOCKADE

Ice storms rarely occur along either side of the Rocky Mountains because these high peaks usually block incoming cold air masses. Sometimes, however, cold air manages to invade areas west of the mountains from inland Canada, or areas east of the mountains from the polar regions of the Northwest. Then, conditions may become ideal for the formation of an ice storm.

FREEZING RAIN

Freezing rain falls only when ice-storm weather conditions continue for at least several hours. If temperatures in either the cold layers or the warm layer change—by even one degree—the storm may produce snow or rain instead of freezing rain. If the moisture level in the air drops, the storm may fizzle out altogether. The **glaze** or **rime** that forms on objects and surfaces in an ice storm represents **precipitation** that has changed and then changed again as it has fallen through a warm-air "sandwich."

Supercooled rain falling on barbed wire coats the fencing in ice.

Snow into rain

The ice begins in clouds as snowflakes or ice crystals. As the snow or ice crystals fall from the cold upper layer through the warmer middle layer—where temperatures are above **freezing point**—they melt completely and become raindrops.

Rain into freezing rain

As the rain falls into the cold lower layer, it remains a liquid because this surface layer is so thin that the drops don't have time to refreeze. Instead, they become **supercooled**—that is, they remain liquid even though their temperature has dropped below freezing point.

Hold the ice

Supercooled water can't turn into ice until it finds a "docking station." In general, ice crystals form when supercooled droplets touch something solid. These solid objects are often microscopic—tiny particles of dust, specks of plant **debris** raised by the wind, or other ice crystals. Supercooled droplets also freeze if they land on a solid surface—a sidewalk or tree branch—chilled to below freezing point. That is why the ice in an ice cube tray forms first around the edges of each compartment and then "grows" toward the center. Without a "docking station," the droplets can remain in liquid form at temperatures as cold as –40 °F (–40 °C).

Freezing rain into ice

When a drop of freezing rain hits a cold surface, it spreads out and freezes solid. Each drop adds a microscopically thin layer of ice to the surface. Over time, many tiny, thin layers build up to create the thick, icy coating characteristic of ice storms.

FREEZING RAIN IS NOT SLEET

Freezing rain and **sleet** are not the same. Sleet bounces and makes a rapping sound when it hits a hard surface. It consists of transparent grains of ice smaller than ⅕ inch (5 millimeters) in diameter. Like freezing rain, sleet can form from supercooled droplets that fall through a warm-air "sandwich." However, if the ice crystals don't melt completely and if the cold lower layer is thick enough, the ice crystals can refreeze before hitting the surface.

A man uses a mallet to break up a layer of glaze ice that has formed on his car.

THE "GREAT BLIZZARD" OF 1951

One of the most damaging ice storms in United States history hit the south-central states in early 1951. **Freezing rain,** sleet, and snow fell across an area more than 100 miles (160 kilometers) wide from Arkansas to Ohio. Nashville, Tennessee, was one of the hardest-hit areas. There, the storm is remembered as the "Great Blizzard."

How it happened

The storm began on Sunday, January 28, with rain that turned to freezing rain then snow as temperatures plummeted. By Monday, Nashville had more than 1½ inches (3.8 centimeters) of snow-covered ice on the ground. On Tuesday, it seemed that the worst was over, but on Wednesday, another 5 inches (13 centimeters) of ice and snow fell. On Thursday, the storm dumped 5 more inches of freezing rain and snow on the besieged city. Then, on Friday, temperatures dropped to -13 °F (-25 °C).

The 1951 ice storm affected an area stretching from Arkansas to Ohio.

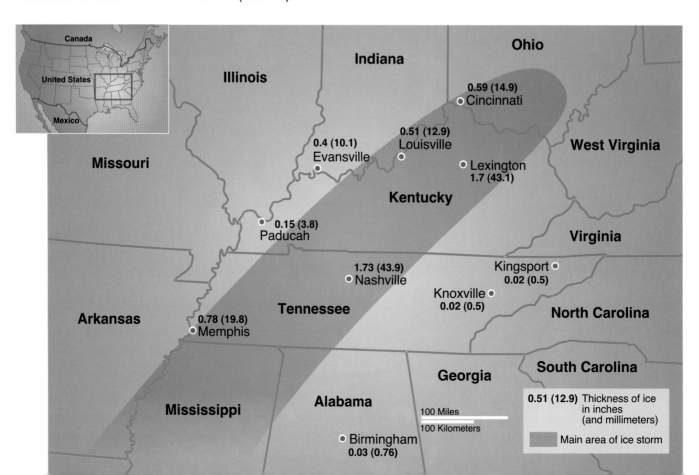

Shutdown

The storm brought Nashville to a standstill. Businesses closed. Airlines canceled flights. The trains that managed to run were up to two days late. So many city buses were stuck in the ice and snow that transit officials in Nashville asked the nearby city of Memphis to send more, but the replacements got stuck on the way. Abandoned cars and trucks clogged city streets. Thousands of fallen trees blocked area roads. City workers and volunteers worked hard to clear roadways, but the ice was so thick even bulldozers failed. One resident recalled, "I set out to go to work on the ice, but 21st Avenue looked like ocean waves the way the snow and ice had fallen and [been] driven by the wind. I just backed it up and called it a day."

Ice and falling trees brought down power lines, leaving more than 80,000 people in and around Nashville without electric power. Telephone lines snapped because of the ice and cold. Roofs collapsed.

Costly ice

The Great Blizzard claimed 25 lives. More than 500 people suffered injuries. The ice ruined many orchards and killed thousands of head of livestock. Experts estimated the cost of the storm at over $100 million.

Trees, weighed down by a thick coating of ice, threaten cars parked on the streets of Nashville, Tennessee, during the Great Blizzard of 1951.

THE JAM AFTER THE THAW

When the thaw began at last, on February 5, thousands of people were finally able to leave their homes. Some set out for work or to visit relatives or to buy food. Others tried to reclaim their abandoned cars. The result was probably the worst traffic jam in Nashville's history. Newspapers reported that main roadways leading to the city were backed up for more than 5 miles (8 kilometers).

THE HUMAN COST

Ice storms are usually not as deadly as other natural disasters. Unlike **tsunamis** or **tornadoes,** they rarely kill people directly. But they still lead to injury and death.

Two students skate to school along a street covered in black ice after an ice storm struck Chicago in 1935.

Icy accidents

Accidents, especially traffic accidents, are usually the main cause of death in ice storms. Drivers need at least 10 times as much roadway to stop on icy roads as they do on dry pavement. Icy sidewalks are perilous for pedestrians.

Trying to remove ice from the roof of a building is a dangerous activity. Sometimes, roofs weighed down with ice collapse on the people inside. People are also killed by breaking tree branches and chunks of ice falling from roofs.

Live wires

As **freezing rain** falls on electric-power lines, the ice begins to coat the wires. The ice may become so heavy that it snaps the lines. Even if downed lines are not sparking or snaking on the ground, electricity may still be traveling through them. Electricity always seeks the easiest path to the ground. If you touch anything along that path, **electric current** will flow through you, causing a potentially fatal shock. Electric current may also travel though tree branches and other objects touching a downed line, including water puddles. Safety experts recommend staying at least 10 feet (16 meters) from any downed **utility** line, even if you think it may be a telephone line.

Indoor dangers

A widespread power outage, known as a **blackout,** brings danger indoors. The candles people use for light sometimes cause deadly fires. Fighting fires is difficult during a storm. Icy streets, fallen branches, and downed electric lines make it difficult for emergency equipment to reach a fire scene.

Dangerous fumes

During cold-weather blackouts, **carbon monoxide** poisoning claims victims. Carbon monoxide is a colorless, odorless gas that is often called the "silent killer." At high levels, it can quickly cause unconsciousness and death. During a blackout, people sometimes try to heat their home using charcoal grills, camp stoves, and other outdoor cooking or heating devices. All these devices give off carbon monoxide.

Portable indoor heating units called space heaters fueled by propane and kerosene—as well as fireplaces that are not properly ventilated—may give off carbon monoxide. Some space heaters have hot surfaces that may cause burns if touched or fires if they are placed too close to drapes and other **flammable** objects.

Ice storms typically result in damage to cars as tree branches break under the enormous weight of ice.

CUT OFF
If utility lines go down, a battery-powered or hand-cranked radio may be the only way to get information about the outside world. Some of these radios can also recharge cell phones.

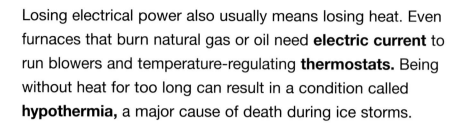

Losing electrical power also usually means losing heat. Even furnaces that burn natural gas or oil need **electric current** to run blowers and temperature-regulating **thermostats.** Being without heat for too long can result in a condition called **hypothermia,** a major cause of death during ice storms.

Dropping temperature

In hypothermia, body temperature falls to less than 95 °F (35 °C). A person whose body temperature falls below 90 °F (32 °C) may lose consciousness. If body temperature drops below about 80 °F (27 °C), the heart may not be able to pump blood properly through the body, and death may result.

Elderly people, small children, and people with medical problems have a higher risk of developing hypothermia, even in relatively warm temperatures. In addition, cool temperatures are not the only risk factor for hypothermia. People who are cold and wet may lose body heat 25 times faster than they would if they were cold and dry. Hypothermia can also result from exposure to wind, which can cool the body faster than the body can produce heat.

The human body has ways of adjusting to abnormally low temperatures. A normal body temperature is 98.6 °F (37 °C) (below left). During hypothermia, when the body is very cold, it diverts heat to the core to try to keep vital organs warm (below right).

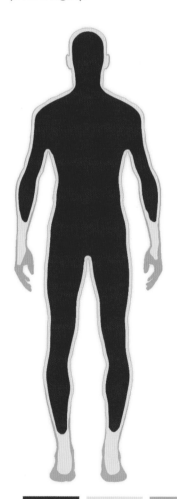
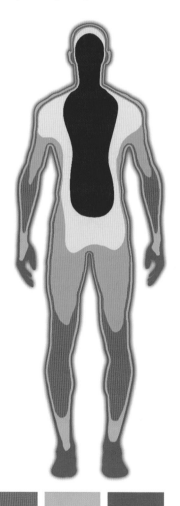

98.6 °F (37 °C)	98.6-96.8 °F (37-36 °C)	96.8-89.6 °F (36-32 °C)	89.6-82.4 °F (32-28 °C)	82.4-77 °F (28-25 °C)	Below 77 °F (25 °C)

What to look for

The first signs of hypothermia usually include changes in a person's ability to control the nerves and muscles, symptoms popularly known as "the umbles." That is, a person in the early stages of hypothermia might *stumble, mumble, fumble,* and *grumble.* Other signs of hypothermia include:

- Shivering
- Skin that looks blue and feels cold and waxy
- Numb hands or fingers
- Slow pulse
- Apparent exhaustion
- Drowsiness

What to do

If you suspect someone has hypothermia:

- Call an ambulance or take the person to a hospital as soon as possible.
- While waiting for help, remove any wet clothing the victim is wearing and wrap him or her in dry blankets.
- Don't apply hot water, hot pads, or other forms of direct heat to the victim.
- Don't rub the victim's arms and legs.
- If the person is awake, give him or her warm—never hot—liquid without alcohol or caffeine, which can increase the loss of body heat.

A boy wears suitable clothes to protect him from the extreme cold of a Russian winter.

FOCUS ON THE CORE

A person with hypothermia should remain still. Moving, heating, or rubbing the victim's arms and legs could push cold blood back to the victim's heart, lungs, and brain. This could cause the person's temperature to drop even lower. It could also cause heart failure. Instead, put warm cloths on the person's chest and abdomen and the sides of the neck to help raise the temperature in the **core.**

THE 1921 ICE STORM

The New England ice storm of 1921 was one of the worst to ever hit that part of the United States. In late November, central and eastern Massachusetts were bombarded by 75 hours of **freezing rain,** rain, **sleet,** and snow blown about by high winds.

Intense ice

Although the storm raged for three days, it did not cover a huge area. In addition to Massachusetts, the storm affected small areas of Rhode Island, Connecticut, and New Hampshire. At least 15 people died. The storm caused more than $50 million—$500 million in 2007 dollars—in damage to trees and to electric and telephone lines.

Tree trauma

In some areas, the **glaze** reached a thickness of at least 3 inches (7.5 centimeters), damaging or destroying almost every tree in the area of the storm. More than 100,000 trees were brought down or badly damaged in Massachusetts alone. The storm ruined many parks and gardens. It was also a terrible blow to New England's tree farmers. The storm cost maple syrup producers millions of dollars. Other commercial trees, such as those in apple orchards, suffered too.

Central and western Massachusetts were hardest hit by the 1921 ice storm.

Canada
United States

50 Miles
50 Kilometers
Area of ice storm

Vermont

Maine

New Hampshire
Concord ●
Manchester ●

Atlantic Ocean

Boston ●

Massachusetts

Providence ●
Hartford ●

Connecticut

Rhode Island

Other effects

Although electric lighting in streets and homes was a relatively new development in the 1920's, New England had miles of electrical cables. Many of these cables were pulled down by falling trees and by the weight of the ice that had collected on them. In one case, an estimated 4 tons (3.6 metric tons) coated the wires between two telephone poles. Workers in Lowell, Massachusetts, had to rebuild the power line to two local hospitals three times because breaking and falling tree branches kept knocking it down.

At sea

The storm sank two ships. It also cut off all radio communication with the Lightship *Nantucket* for 13 hours. Floating lighthouses, lightships were anchored at dangerous places to warn and guide ships. Anchored off Nantucket Island, the Lightship *Nantucket* monitored the main transit point for ships crossing the North Atlantic between the United States and Europe.

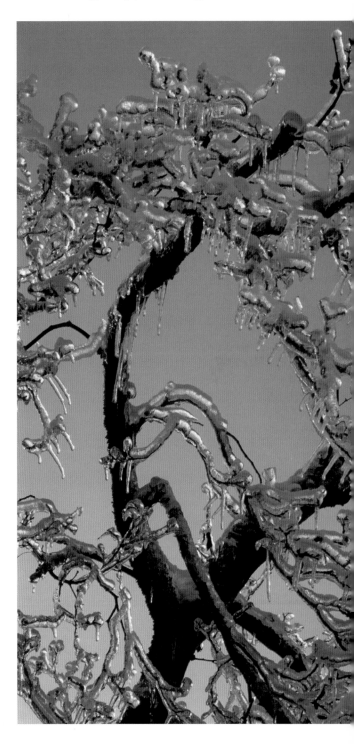

Like most ice storms, the New England storm of 1921 destroyed and damaged hundreds of thousands of trees, ruining many parks and gardens.

A 1920'S VIEW

The Lowell Electric Light Corporation produced a booklet describing the effects of the storm and the efforts the company made to repair the damage. It said, "... every twig, branch, tree, wire and pole which was exposed to the rain and snow was after a few hours coated with a load of ice far beyond anything which Nature had provided against and man had met in his experience. And, as if Nature was trying to outdo herself, on Tuesday morning, November 29, there was a thunder storm."

THE EL NIÑO EFFECT

El Niño is a disruption in the normal way Earth's **atmosphere** and the **tropical** waters of the Pacific Ocean interact. This event, which occurs every two to seven years, affects weather around the world. Some **meteorologists** believe El Niño also increases the risk of ice storms.

Sea change

The term *El Niño* originally referred to a **current** of warm water that flows southward along the coasts of Ecuador and Peru every winter. During years without an El Niño, the winds of the tropical Pacific blow surface waters from the east—near South America—west toward Southeastern Asia.

During an El Niño event Pacific winds, which usually blow from east to west (top), weaken; waters off South America become much warmer and rainfall shifts eastward (bottom).

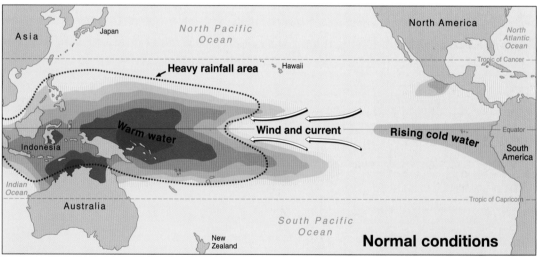

During an El Niño, these tropical winds weaken—or even reverse. The El Niño current becomes abnormally strong and lasts for an unusually long time, about 18 months. As a result, the waters off Ecuador and Peru become abnormally warm.

Rain and drought

Because the water is so warm, higher-than-normal amounts of **water vapor** are pumped into the air over North and South America. During an El Niño, the coast of South America becomes wetter than normal. By contrast, the climate in Southeast Asia becomes unusually dry. **Droughts** may even occur.

El Niños and ice storms

Some meteorologists think that the atmospheric changes caused by an El Niño make it more likely that warm and cold **air masses** will mix over eastern North America and so produce more ice storms. They believe that an El Niño played a role in the Great Ice Storm of 1998 that devastated parts of the United States and Canada. This El Niño, which began in the spring of 1997, became the strongest of these events in at least 50 years. Some meteorologists have argued that an El Niño pushed the section of the **jet stream** that normally blows across the southern part of the United States north into the Canadian provinces of Ontario and Quebec. As the jet stream raced north, it flooded southeastern Canada with warm, moist air. Other meteorologists, however, have argued that the conditions that led to the storm were too complicated to be certain that El Niño played a major role.

A satellite image of sea temperatures during the El Niño event of 1997 shows the warmest water (in white) gathering off the coast of South America and the southwestern United States.

EL NIÑO'S NAME

The name *El Niño* is Spanish for *the boy* and is often used to refer to the Christ child. South Americans gave this name to the warm ocean current that flows along the coast of Ecuador and Peru because it usually arrives in December, just before Christmas.

THE GREAT ICE STORM OF 1998

In January 1998, a devastating ice storm hammered eastern Canada and the northeastern United States. The storm, which lasted from January 4 to 10, ranks as the worst natural disaster in Canada's history. It caused an estimated $5 billion worth of damage—more than any other ice storm in history.

The big one

The ice storm covered an unusually large area and lasted for an unusually long time. It also dumped twice as much **precipitation** as any previous storm had on the region. Normally, **freezing rain** falls for a few hours at a time. In 1998, it poured for a full 80 hours. In many places, the **glaze** grew to 4 inches (10 centimeters) thick.

Blackout

The storm deprived at least 5 million people of electric power in the dead of winter. In Canada, the south shore of Quebec, near Montreal, became known as the "Triangle of Darkness." Some residents of this area had no power until February 6.

During the ice storm of 1998, areas of southeastern Canada and the northeastern United States were blanketed by ice more than 1½ inches (4 centimeters) thick. Accumulation grew to nearly 4 inches (10 centimeters) in some areas.

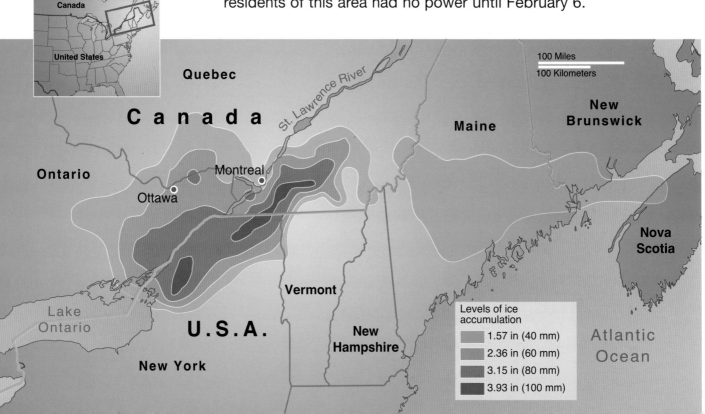

Levels of ice accumulation

- 1.57 in (40 mm)
- 2.36 in (60 mm)
- 3.15 in (80 mm)
- 3.93 in (100 mm)

Death toll

The storm killed at least 28 people in Canada and 17 in the United States. Accidents claimed about one-third of the victims. Almost as many died from **fumes** given off by faulty or makeshift heaters. Other victims died from **hypothermia** or from falls while trying to remove ice and snow from rooftops. Some were killed in fires sparked by candles or overheated fireplaces.

Experts believe the death toll was actually much higher. Many people, especially the elderly, died shortly after the storm because they were weakened by hypothermia or had caught influenza while living in crowded temporary shelters.

Finding shelter

At least 100,000 people were forced to seek refuge in the hundreds of temporary shelters set up in schools, community centers, and other public places. In Montreal, police went door to door to find people who were without heat. They were also given the power to order residents from their home. In one case, officers firmly escorted a man in summer shorts from his apartment after he refused to shut down the barbecue grill he was using for warmth.

Montrealers try to negotiate their way through a maze of broken branches and downed power lines after ice storms hit the city and plunged many homes into darkness and cold.

A LONELY NIGHT

When the power went out, Montreal resident Jennifer Wei took her children to stay with a friend who had a heating stove, then came back to guard her own house. She described spending the night beside a tiny fire: "It was an endless night for me. I was solitary in a freezing room, surrounded by darkness and quietness. Only the flame and a book accompanied me. ... I fell asleep with tiredness and was awakened by coldness continuously."

An ice coating weighing in the tons crumples steel power transmission towers in Canada during the great storm of 1998. Only one of five transmission stations supplying Montreal with electric power remained operational.

Sights and sounds

During the 1998 storm, exploding power **transformers** and electric arcs lit the sky. The sounds of snapping **utility** wires and the cracking and crashing of tree branches filled the air.

Light show

The **freezing rain** attacked every outdoor surface, including huge steel transmission towers, which distribute high-voltage **electric current** produced in power plants. Burdened by at least twice the weight of ice they were designed to withstand, the towers toppled like dominos. Only one of the five main transmission stations that supplied Montreal and surrounding communities remained standing. Throughout the storm area, crushed and twisted towers littered the frozen ground like abandoned toys.

The ice also dragged down at least 30,000 wooden utility poles. Sparks of brilliant blue and orange light signaled the explosions of power transformers, which help transfer current to homes and businesses. Even more frightening were the brilliant arcs of blue-green light leaping from damaged electric wires as current was transformed into light.

Storm sounds

One resident of Quebec described the sound of the storm:

"... the morning calm was regularly punctuated by the sound of cracking and breaking branches. First there was a sharp crack, then the clinking sound magnified a thousand fold as the branch fell through the tree, followed by a crash as it hit the hard ice layer on the ground, then the sound of breaking glass as the ice shards scattered in every direction."

A man hiking along the Wapack Trail in New Hampshire after the storm e-mailed a conservation group that, "The air was filled with the sound of ice-laden branches swayed by the wind and the constant clatter of ice debris falling through the trees. I ... beat a hasty retreat in consideration of grapefruit sized chunks of ice and heavy branches occasionally thumping to the ground nearby me."

THE SILVER THAW

Newfoundland, on Canada's eastern coast, gets up to three times as much freezing rain as any other Canadian province—an average of 150 hours each winter. In Newfoundland, the coating of ice created by freezing rain is known as *silver thaw*. According to one humorous story explaining the origin of the term, early European immigrants to Newfoundland expected to become rich quickly by gathering silver from the trees. Instead, they discovered that the "silver" was really ice.

The residents of Montreal, which had suffered through the 1998 storm, were hit again in 2005 with an ice storm that left large areas of the city without electric power.

Animals in the storm

Animals suffered during the storm. More than 20,000 farms lost power. Farmers could not keep their livestock warm or pump fresh water for them to drink. Thousands of animals died. Many animals died when barn or shed roofs collapsed under the weight of the ice.

Farmers could not milk their cows because milking machines run on electric power. Milk processing plants were shut, and about 2.6 million gallons (10 million liters) of milk worth some $6 million was dumped in Ontario alone. Farmers in the United States lost $12.7 million worth of milk.

ON THE FARM

Ontario dairy farmer Connie McDiarmid explained some of the problems that face farmers when they lose their power supply: "With herds of 50 cows and more, one cannot begin to milk by hand. It would take probably half an hour for a top-producing cow, and after one cow the farmer's hands would be cramping and sore. Farmers are not used to this and neither are the cows. ..."

A farmer connects one of his cows up to a milking machine.

At the zoo

Zookeepers at the Granby Zoo southeast of Montreal scrambled to keep animal residents warm, according to one newspaper report. Keepers moved the flamingos in with the elephants. They ran portable **generators** to keep the alligators from freezing. One of their biggest challenges was feeding the exotic birds, which eat only in bright light. Battery-powered lights turned on at lunchtime saved the day. During the ice storm, a lioness from a Louisiana zoo arrived to take up residency at the zoo. Zookeepers named her Gresil, which means hail.

Trees

The storm took a severe toll on trees and other plantlife, bringing down millions of trees. Up to 70 percent of the forests in the four U.S. states struck by the storm suffered some damage. Even after the storm, trees weakened by the ice broke and fell through the rest of the winter. Loggers, sawmill owners, and other workers in the timber industry lost millions of dollars.

The crushing ice destroyed or severely damaged most of Quebec's domestic maple trees, from which producers collect maple syrup. Quebec produces about 70 percent of the world's supply of this sweet liquid. Millions of taps (drainage spouts in maple trees) were buried. An association of maple syrup producers in Ontario estimated that it could take 40 years for production in the eastern part of the province to return to normal. Maple syrup producers in New York also suffered devastating losses.

A bucket is used to collect the sweet sap of a maple tree, from which maple syrup is made. The 1998 ice storm crippled Quebec's maple syrup industry.

Rescue operations

The 1998 ice storm was so huge and powerful that it would have taken local people years to repair everything by themselves. Instead, thousands of volunteers, military personnel, and electric company workers from across Canada and the United States came to help.

Operation Recuperation

On January 8, the Canadian Forces went into action with a rescue operation code-named Operation Recuperation. More than 15,000 personnel were assigned to a range of tasks. Soldiers rescued sick and injured people and animals, cleared roads for emergency vehicles, set up emergency shelters, and delivered emergency food and water supplies. They also helped farmers by delivering and repairing **generators,** which turn fuel into electric power. It was one of the largest military operations in modern Canadian history. The bill for the operation was $60 million.

Emergency teams remove accumulated ice and snow in Montreal after the 1998 ice storm.

Power repairs

Once emergency needs had been met, the next task was to repair electric cables, towers, and wooden **utility** poles. Line-repair crews—who are trained to work with power lines—arrived from all over the country. Military engineers and technical staff also used their specialist knowledge to help. But the damage was so bad that many towers and cables could not be repaired. They had to be removed and replaced.

Line-repair crews from as far away as Hawaii work to fix power cables and towers damaged by the 1998 ice storm.

Lengthy effort

Even with extra workers, the armed forces, and volunteers helping out, it took months to return the electric supply system to normal. Three weeks after the storm, 700,000 people were still without power. There were other kinds of damage too—collapsed roofs and sheds, crushed cars, and burst pipes.

HELP FROM HAWAII

Line-repair crews came from as far away as Hawaii to help reconnect power cables in New England. They described their experiences of the storm:

"When we're home and there's a power outage, well, the air conditioners don't work. But here when the power goes off, there's no heat and you can die. It makes us feel that we're really doing something very important."
—Hipo Pincena

"And to think I was surfing on Thursday. ... This is cold. This is really cold. It really gives you an appreciation for the beach." —Chris Acoba

SURVIVING AN ICE STORM

Staying safe in an ice storm depends on being well prepared and knowing how to stay warm, avoid the most common dangers, and deal with emergencies.

Being prepared

If an ice storm may be on the way, officials with emergency preparedness agencies advise people to fill the gas tanks of their automobiles to keep ice from forming in the tank or fuel line. Stock up on such high-energy foods as nuts, dried fruit, and granola bars and on foods that do not require refrigeration or cooking, such as canned beans and soups. Supplies should include a minimum three-day supply of water that includes 1 gallon (3.8 liters) of water per person per day. (Be sure to have water available for pets.) Other essentials to have on hand include:

- A battery-powered National Oceanic and Atmospheric Administration (NOAA) weather radio, which can receive warnings and forecasts from the National Weather Service
- A flashlight and extra batteries or a hand-crank flashlight that does not require batteries
- Candles and waterproof matches
- An extra supply of prescription drugs and commonly used over-the-counter medication
- Blankets and sleeping bags
- Warm clothes, socks, and knitted hats
- Baby supplies (diapers, food, formula), if needed.

A man ventures out during an ice storm to collect wood to use as fuel to keep warm.

Staying warm

To stay warm, have an emergency heat source that runs without electric power—a wood stove, a fireplace, or a space heater—and a fuel supply. Make sure that such devices are ventilated properly and that a **carbon monoxide** detector is installed nearby.

Another way to keep warm is to huddle together in one room. Wear several layers of clothing. Wrap up in warm blankets, sleeping bags, or comforters. Try to stay dry.

Stuff paper or towels under gaps at the bottom of doors. Cover windows at night to prevent heat loss. Watch for the early signs of **hypothermia.**

Montreal residents eat by candlelight during an ice-storm blackout. People living in areas prone to ice storms need to keep an emergency supply of candles.

Avoiding common dangers

When an ice storm cuts off power and communications, it is tempting to go out to seek help—or even to admire the ice. However, the safest place during an ice storm is indoors, as long as you are properly protected and supplied. If not, local or state agencies usually set up temporary shelters in schools, churches, community centers, and other public places.

Drink adequate amounts of fluid to prevent **dehydration,** but avoid caffeine and alcohol.

Be sure smoke detectors are functioning. Have a fire extinguisher handy. Don't burn candles near drapes, furniture, or other **flammable** materials. Don't leave burning candles unattended.

DEALING WITH EMERGENCIES

Keep a first-aid kit with your emergency supplies. If you must leave your house, don't travel alone. Let someone else know your route, destination, and estimated time of arrival. Drive or walk carefully to avoid slipping accidents. Make sure your car is equipped with a winter storm survival kit that includes a first-aid kit, extra clothing, flashlight and batteries, a tow rope, and sack of sand or cat litter for traction.

THE CHRISTMAS 2000 ICE STORM

Over the Christmas holiday in 2000, an ice storm crippled a large area of the south-central United States. The storm, which affected Arkansas, Louisiana, Oklahoma, and Texas, claimed more than 40 lives. To make matters worse, the Christmas storm was the second ice storm to hit the region during that month. A smaller ice storm on December 12 and 13 had knocked out electric power to 250,000 people in the region, some of whom then lived under **blackout** conditions for 10 days. The Christmas storm hit just two days after 7,000 extra electric company workers called in to fix lines downed in the first storm had finally gone home.

A street sign marks the entrance to Sunshine, Texas, a town that is more used to warm weather than ice storms.

Winter weather

The storm began on Christmas Eve with **freezing rain.** Many places were soon struggling with 1 to 3 inches (2.5 to 7.5 centimeters) of ice. In some places, the **glaze** was up to 6 inches (15 centimeters) thick.

Losses

The sound of tree branches snapping soon echoed through the air. Electric wires as well as the transmission towers that carried them started coming down. About 600,000 people in the four states found themselves in a holiday blackout.

A DIFFERENT KIND OF HOLIDAY

A father from Little Rock, Arkansas, described his family's experience. "We lit half a dozen candles and played *Clue* by candlelight. ... It's an extended Christmas. That's how I'm looking at it."

Arkansas Governor Mike Huckabee said his state had had "an electrical heart attack."

Farmers, especially Arkansas' many chicken farmers, suffered major losses from the storm. The American Red Cross and crews of United States military personnel delivered emergency **generators** to farmers to help them keep their chicken sheds warm. The glaze severely damaged about 40 percent of the state's timberland, an area equal to the size of Los Angeles.

No water

During the storm, at least 120,000 people in 35 Arkansas cities found their water supply dwindling to a trickle. Because of the blackout, water plants couldn't treat and pump water to customers. Some people hauled water from streams and ponds for their pets.

Residents of Hot Springs, Arkansas, were more fortunate than most. Carrying bottles and jugs, they lined up at public fountains fed by the city's world-famous mineral springs. For a while, the springs provided the only running water in the city. A company that bottles water from a spring near the city shipped water to Hot Springs hospitals.

The many spring-fed fountains and baths in Hot Springs, Arkansas, supplied the famous resort's residents with their only source of fresh water during the Christmas ice storm of 2000.

Glaze ice coats a pecan tree in Oklahoma during the 2000 ice storm. Pecan nuts are a major crop in the south-central United States, and the storm devastated many pecan groves.

The Christmas Ice Storm paralyzed transportation throughout much of the South. Holiday travelers added to the confusion. Many people trying to visit family and friends were left stranded. Road conditions were so perilous that the United States Postal Service halted mail deliveries in the hardest-hit areas.

Roads to chaos

The ice storm turned thousands of roads, including Interstate 40 in Oklahoma and Arkansas, into ice rinks. Cars skidded and crashed, and heavy trucks slipped and slid sideways as they tried to climb icy hills. Traffic lights went dark, adding to the confusion.

The ice, fallen trees, accidents, and downed **utility** lines blocked many roads completely. Some traffic jams extended for 15 miles (24 kilometers), leaving thousands of people stranded in their cars. Governor Mike Huckabee ordered members of the National Guard in military all-terrain vehicles called Humvees to search for people trapped in their homes or cars. All across the region, buses and trains were canceled. Many people had to turn back or spend the holiday in motels or in emergency shelters set up in schools, gyms, and churches.

Air agony

The ice storm made air travel a nightmare. The Dallas/Fort Worth Airport in Texas, a major hub for flights to and from the South, canceled hundreds of flights. The Little Rock airport shut down for three days because of **glaze** on the runways. The airports filled up with frustrated and exhausted passengers waiting to hear if they could take off soon—only to find flight after flight canceled.

An airplane stands in an ice-bound airport. The Christmas Ice Storm shut down airports across the south-central United States.

Standstill

With roads shut down, supplies of fuel and fresh food began to run out. In Texarkana, Arkansas, which was totally cut off, an emergency rule banned storekeepers from raising prices to take advantage of the panic caused by the ice storm.

Clean up

After the storm ended, 25,000 workers, including 10,000 line-repair workers from 25 states, labored for 3 weeks to repair 7 million feet (2.1 million meters) of downed electric lines and replace 4,136 utility poles. There were so many workers that the electric company booked 14,000 rooms in 554 hotels so they had somewhere to stay.

CHRISTMAS BOMB

The Christmas Ice Storm was the most damaging ice storm in Arkansas history. That storm and the storm earlier in the month together caused more than $547 million in damage. Governor Huckabee said the storm was "really the equivalent of having a nuclear device go off without the mushroom cloud or radioactivity. We [had] 11 or 12 counties where every single person [had] lost power, phone service, and water."

FORECASTING ICE STORMS

Ice storms are hard to forecast because the weather conditions that produce them are so specific and can change so easily. However, weather-forecasting technology is always improving, and **meteorologists** are getting better at predicting when and where ice storms will happen.

Meteorologists launch a weather balloon to carry weather-measuring devices into the atmosphere.

Collecting data

The first step in forecasting an ice storm is to determine weather conditions. Meteorologists often send up **weather balloons** with a package of measuring devices, called a **radiosonde,** attached to them. The radiosonde records the temperature, **air pressure,** and **humidity** at different **altitudes.** This information can reveal when layers of warm and cold air are building up in a way that could cause an ice storm.

Meteorologists also use **satellites** and **radar** to follow the weather. Satellites orbiting Earth can detect heat energy, so they can map warm and cold **air masses.** Radar equipment sends out radio waves, which bounce off clouds and **water vapor** in the air, showing where they are.

Computer power

Once meteorologists have collected their data, the information is fed into a powerful computer system. The computer creates a model showing the location of various air masses and how fast they are moving, and

then calculates where they will go next. If the conditions for an ice storm are likely, the computer can show roughly where and when it will happen and how much ice is likely to form.

A meteorologist studies weather patterns across the United States using a bank of computer screens.

Ice storm warning

When an ice storm is predicted, government weather services issue a warning. It is broadcast on television and radio, reported in the newspapers, and posted on the Internet. In addition to giving information about when and where an ice storm may strike, warnings remind people how to stay safe during the storm. They warn the public to stay indoors and off the roads and to make sure they have a store of fuel and food ready in case their power is cut off.

READY TO ACT

Members of the public aren't the only people who need to know if an ice storm is on the way. The **utility** companies, city and state governments, hospitals, and emergency services also rely on weather forecasts. They use them to plan how many staff they will need in case of an emergency.

THE MIDWEST ICE STORM OF 2006

Cars travel slowly on narrow pathways along Interstate 35 in Wichita, Kansas, during the 2006 ice storm.

One of the worst ice storms to hit the Midwest in nearly 30 years began innocently. On Nov. 29, 2006, temperatures in parts of Missouri and Illinois reached an unseasonably warm 72 °F (22 °C). Even then weather forecasters warned that a storm was approaching.

Drop in temperature

The storm began with rain about 7 a.m. on November 30. The rain turned into **sleet, freezing rain,** and ice as the temperature dropped by 46 degrees during the following 36 hours. A low-pressure system kept warm air hovering in the area, preventing the freezing rain from becoming snow until nightfall.

Ice and snow

In some areas, 2 inches (5 centimeters) of ice accumulated on tree branches and power lines. The ice was topped by up to 18 inches (46 centimeters) of snow. On the night of November 30, residents—particularly those along the direct path of the storm from Jackson, Missouri, in the southwest to Pontiac, Illinois, in the northeast—were repeatedly startled awake by the snapping of tree limbs, the crashing of **utility** poles, and the power bursts from downed power lines. Nearly 500,000 customers from Texas to Michigan lost power, and some did not regain it for an entire week.

Life at a standstill

By December 1, thousands of airline passengers were stranded, highways were blocked with abandoned vehicles, and trains were stalled because of signal problems caused by **blackouts.** Thousands of people abandoned their homes for warming shelters. National Guard troops in Illinois and Missouri went door to door, checking to be sure that people who had stayed in their homes were safe without heat and electric power.

A POWER PROBLEM

As with many modern ice storms, the danger in the 2006 Midwest storm came primarily from the blackouts that it caused. St. Louis-based utility Ameren Corp., which provides power to the area, had installed 391 miles (629 kilometers) of wire by December 7 in an effort to restore power. However, high winds and tree limbs that continued to break and fall brought power lines down as fast as the workers could repair them. By December 7, 20,000 customers were still without power.

Death and destruction

At least 23 people died from storm-related causes. In addition, many farmers lost animals and crops. In central Missouri, the heavy snow caused 16 poultry barns to collapse, killing some 20,000 turkeys. The snow was also responsible for the collapse of a number of hay barns and a dairy operation. Early estimates of the storm damage totaled more than $8 million.

Illinois Army National Guardsmen make house-to-house stops to check on the safety of residents in Decatur, Illinois, during the ice storm of 2006.

ACTIVITY

Make freezing rain

Freezing rain turns into ice when **supercooled** water touches a freezing surface. It's hard to make supercooled water at home or in the classroom, but you may be able to get it cold enough to make a small amount of freezing rain.

Equipment

- Clean plastic plant-spray bottle
- Plastic wrap
- Water (**distilled water** works better than tap water)
- A few large pebbles, a roof shingle, or a ceramic tile
- A freezer

Instructions

1. Place the pebbles, shingle, or tile in the freezer.

2. Set the spray top on the bottle at "fine spray." (You may need to put some water in the bottle to check the setting.) Then take off the spray top and leave the bottle to dry.

3. Fill the bottle with clean or distilled water. Cover the top with plastic wrap and leave the bottle at room temperature for a few hours.

4. Carefully move the bottle into the freezer, without moving or shaking it. After a few more hours, take it out. At least some of the water should still be liquid.

5. Take out the frozen pebbles. Remove the plastic wrap from the bottle and put the spray top back onto the bottle. Spray the supercooled water on the pebbles, shingle, or tile. Watch a thin sheet of ice form.

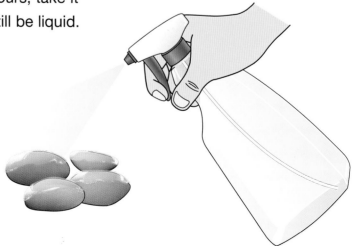

air mass A large body of air at a particular temperature, humidity, and height.

air pressure Pressure caused by the weight of the air in Earth's atmosphere.

altitude Height above Earth's surface or sea level.

atmosphere The layer of gases surrounding Earth.

black ice Very smooth ice that is hard to see when it forms on roads.

blackout A complete loss of electric power.

blizzard A heavy snowstorm with high winds.

carbon monoxide A colorless, odorless, and tasteless gas that is very poisonous if breathed in by people.

condense To change a gas or vapor into liquid by cooling.

core The center, or central part, of something.

curfew A period of time during which the inhabitants of a city or other area are restricted to their homes.

current A flow of water or air in a particular direction.

debris Rubble, broken objects, or other damaged material.

dehydration A condition characterized by the excessive loss of water from the body.

dense Closely packed together.

distilled water Water that has been evaporated, then cooled to form liquid water again in order to remove impurities.

drought A long period of unusually dry weather.

electric current The flow of electrical charges through conductors.

El Niño A part of the interaction between Earth's atmosphere and the tropical waters of the Pacific Ocean that occurs every two to seven years and can affect the climate throughout the world.

evaporate To change from a liquid into a vapor.

flammable Easily set on fire.

freezing point The temperature at which a liquid freezes, 32 °F (0 °C).

freezing rain Rain made up of supercooled raindrops that freeze solid when they touch a cold surface.

friction The property objects have that makes them resist being moved across one another.

frost Water vapor near the ground that freezes into ice crystals that form patterns on exposed surfaces.

fumes Vapors, gases, or smoke given off by something, such as burning fuel.

generator A machine that converts mechanical energy into electrical energy.

glaze A glassy coating of ice formed by freezing rain landing on cold surfaces.

humidity The amount of moisture in the air.

hypothermia A dangerous condition caused by a person's body temperature falling too low, usually below 95 °F (35 °C).

jet stream A band of fast-moving air currents high in Earth's atmosphere.

lubricant A substance that makes moving parts smooth and slippery to allow them to move against one another.

meteorologist Someone who studies and forecasts weather.

molecules The smallest particles into which a substance can be divided without chemical change.

precipitation Rain, snow, dew, or other moisture forming out of the air.

predator An animal that hunts and eats other animals.

radar An electronic instrument that allows weather forecasters to locate areas of rain or snow and track the motion of air in a weather system.

radiosonde An instrument carried into the air by a weather balloon to measure weather conditions.

reptile A cold-blooded animal with a dry, scaly skin that breathes by means of lungs.

rime White, crumbly ice formed when fog touches icy-cold surfaces.

satellite An object that continually orbits Earth or some other body in space. People use artificial satellites for such tasks as collecting data.

sleet A type of precipitation formed from small grains of ice.

supercooled Describes a liquid that has cooled to below its normal freezing point without freezing.

thermostat A device that helps control the temperature of an indoor area or of an appliance.

tornado A rapidly rotating column of air that forms under a thundercloud or a developing thundercloud.

transformer A device that increases or decreases the amount of an electric current.

tropical To do with the tropics, the regions of Earth that lie immediately north and south of the equator, between the tropics of Cancer and Capricorn.

tsunami A series of powerful ocean waves produced by an earthquake, landslide, volcanic eruption, or asteroid impact.

urban To do with a city or town.

utility A service such as water, electric power, or gas supply.

water vapor Water in the form of a gas.

weather balloon A balloon designed to rise through the atmosphere carrying instruments for measuring the weather at high altitudes.

weather system A particular set of weather conditions in Earth's atmosphere, which affects a certain area or region for a period of time.

BOOKS

Blizzards and Ice Storms, by Maria Rosado, Simon Spotlight, 1999.

The Ice Storm: An Historic Record in Photographs of January 1998, by Mark Abley, McClelland & Stewart, 1998.

Ice Storm! The 1998 Freeze (X-Treme Disasters that Changed America), by Bob Temple, Bearport Publishing, 2006.

Natural Disasters: Ice Storms, by Anne Ylvisaker, Capstone Press, 2003.

Stories from the Ice Storm, edited by Mark Abley, McClelland & Stewart, 1999.

WEB SITES

http://weather.com/encyclopedia/winter/ice.html

http://www.islandnet.com/~see/weather/doctor.htm

http://www.nws.noaa.gov/om/brochures/wntrstm.htm

http://www.weatherwizkids.com/winter_storms.htm

INDEX